Major Forces in the World Economy:
Concerns for International Business

by John Hein
Director, International Economics

A Research Report from The Conference Board

Contents

Foreword 5

World Trade 6

    Charts: Growth of World Exports 6
                World Exports by Origin and Destination 7
                Growth of Exports by Major Category 9
                Shares in World Exports 9
                Direction of Trade, 1979 11
                Dependence on Foreign Trade 13

International Payments 14

    Charts: International Reserves 15
                Global Current-Account Balances 17
                Foreign-Exchange Rates 19
                External Debt of Non-OPEC Developing Countries 20
                Non-OPEC Countries' External Debt in Perspective 21

Energy 22

    Charts: Composition of World Primary Energy Supply 22
                Primary Energy Production and Consumption by
                    Country Group 23
                Relative Energy Prices to Final Users 25

Multinational Corporations 26

    Charts: The World's 100 and 500 Largest Industrial
                  Corporations by Nationality 27
                500 Largest Industrial Corporations—Number of
                  Companies, by Sales 29
                Combined Sales of 100 Largest U.S. and 100 Largest
                  Non-U.S. Industrial Corporations 30

Foreword

As the world's business leaders gather in San Francisco in September, 1981, for the International Industrial Conference, the seventh of a series initiated in 1957, the problems and issues confronting the world economy appear to be even more numerous and more complex than at the most recent of these meetings four years ago.

These problems and issues—of which worldwide inflation, low levels of economic activity, a slowdown in the growth of world trade, and the energy situation are the most tangible—are affecting virtually every country and all aspects of international economic relations. Moreover, as the countries of the world have become more interdependent, such disturbances are felt more quickly and more widely than was the case, say, twenty years ago. At the same time, the growing degree of economic interdependence and the increasing complexities of domestic policy objectives often make for tension between international economic considerations and a country's domestic policy goals.

It is difficult to keep these manifold developments in proper perspective and to sort out all the forces that today shape the international economic environment. This report focuses on only a few—trade, payments, energy and the multinationals—that have an important bearing on world economic growth and, therefore, are of concern to international business.

This report was prepared in the Economic Research Division, Edgar R. Fiedler, Vice President.

KENNETH A. RANDALL
President

World Trade

It seems to be generally agreed that in the 1980's the world—and the industrial countries in particular—will not achieve the rates of growth in output and trade that had marked the first few decades following World War II. Changes in the patterns of demand and production, the gradual decline in productivity growth, severe limitations on the ability to cope with inflation, and the high cost of developing alternative sources of energy are bound to ensure lower rates of economic growth in the industrial economies, at least for the remainder of this century.

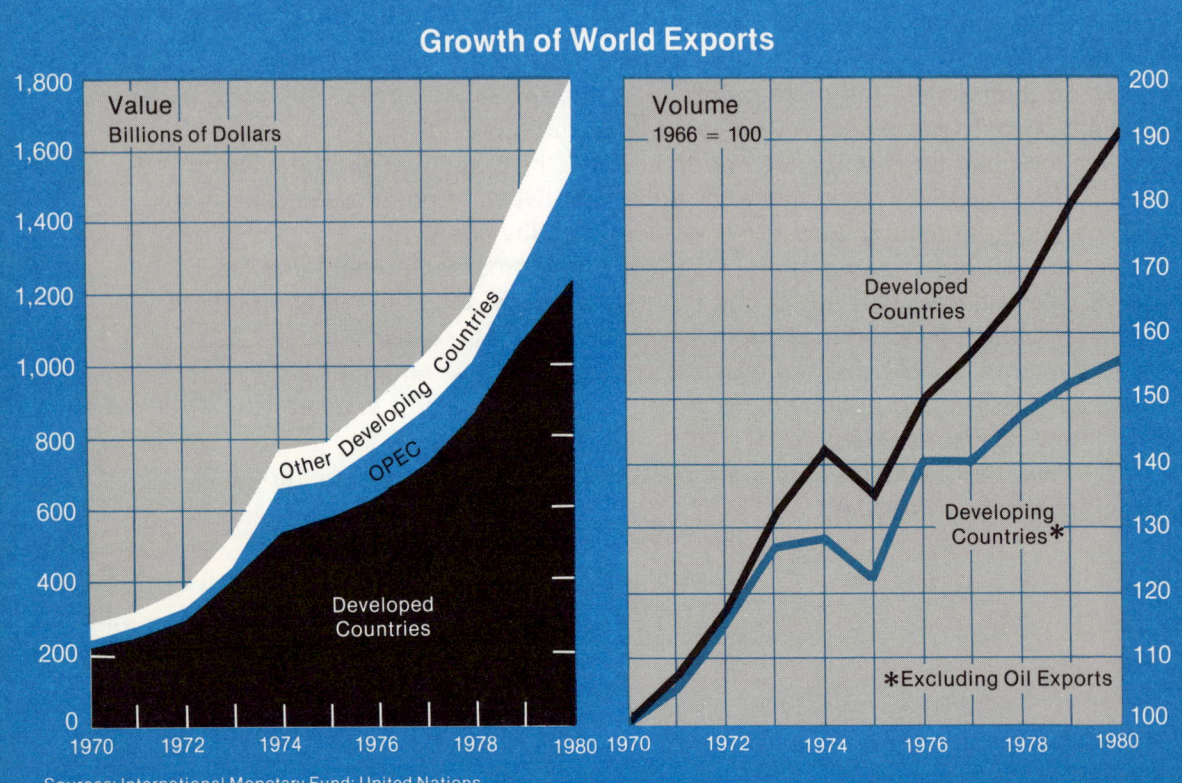

Sources: International Monetary Fund; United Nations

Moreover, the world economy has become increasingly interdependent and there is no longer the expectation that a strong impulse somewhere among the economies of the developing countries might compensate in part for slow growth in the industrial world. No matter how the structure of the world economy is analyzed, its various component parts are functioning more and more like the parts of a machine. As one observer has said: "If one gear slows down, others also slacken." This meshing of gears is particularly pronounced in the case of international trade.

World Exports by Origin and Destination, 1970 & 1979

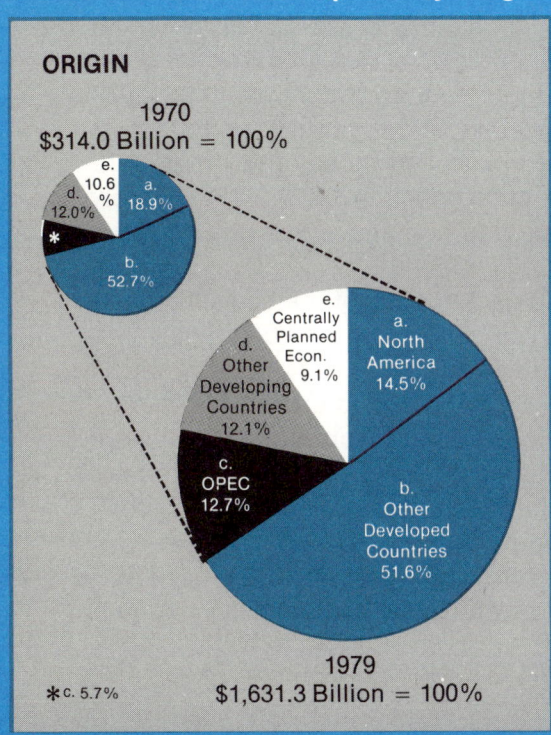

ORIGIN

1970
$314.0 Billion = 100%
- a. 18.9%
- b. 52.7%
- d. 12.0%
- e. 10.6%
- *

1979
$1,631.3 Billion = 100%
- a. North America 14.5%
- b. Other Developed Countries 51.6%
- c. OPEC 12.7%
- d. Other Developing Countries 12.1%
- e. Centrally Planned Econ. 9.1%
- *c. 5.7%

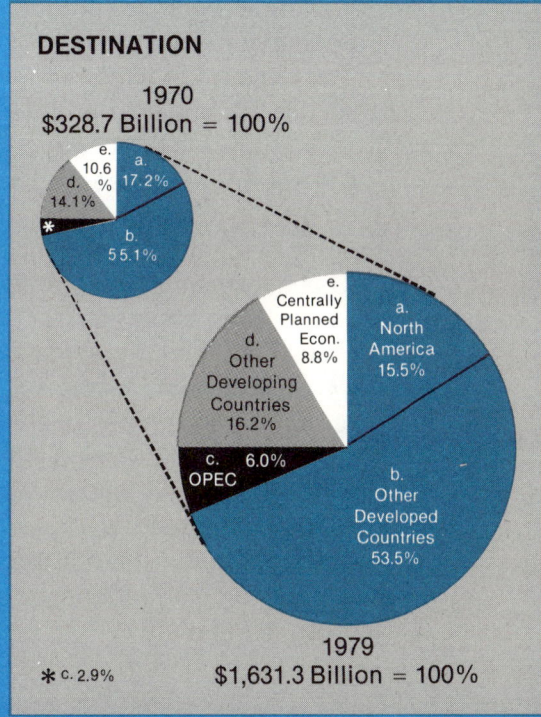

DESTINATION

1970
$328.7 Billion = 100%
- a. 17.2%
- b. 55.1%
- d. 14.1%
- e. 10.6%
- *

1979
$1,631.3 Billion = 100%
- a. North America 15.5%
- b. Other Developed Countries 53.5%
- c. OPEC 6.0%
- d. Other Developing Countries 16.2%
- e. Centrally Planned Econ. 8.8%
- *c. 2.9%

Finally, some analysts think that the world may slowly be running out of resources, that the period of relative resource abundance is over, and that the world economy—with more and more people—must adapt itself to do with less. This applies not only to fossil fuels; the same or similar questions have been raised about the continued availability of such other vital resources as water.

Even more immediately, the accumulation of large trade surpluses by the members of OPEC, discussed in the following section, implies payments deficits in the rest of the world. These not only inhibit the use of expansionary economic policies, but also can induce volatile movements of funds that tend to destabilize exchange rates and thereby make a consistent policy stance more difficult. Some major industrial countries, moreover, that formerly were in surplus have had to cope with payments deficits and thus can no longer be counted on to act as "locomotives" to fuel the growth of world output and trade.

The generally sluggish demand expected by the industrial countries throughout the 1980's and beyond will have unfavorable effects on the exports, particularly of primary commodities, of the developing countries (LDC's). Even excluding fuels, exports of primary commodities account for about 35 percent of LDC merchandise exports and have grown roughly in line with economic activity in the industrial world. There is little reason to expect this relationship to change, especially as imports of certain agricultural products remain limited by protection in Western Europe and Japan.

The outlook for exports of manufactures from the developing world is considered somewhat brighter. In fact, in 1979 exports of manufactures from *all* non-oil developing countries exceeded those of raw materials for the first time. Since the first oil price shock in 1973—which largely prompted this export drive—LDC exports of manufactures have grown at roughly twice the pace of those of raw materials.

This development also reflects the emergence of the so-called newly industrializing countries (NIC's), which generally have been highly selective in their concentration on individual products and markets. The new-found strength of the NIC's was demonstrated earlier this year, when the United States excluded five of them—Hong Kong, South Korea, Taiwan, Brazil and Mexico—from the generalized system of preferences under which, within certain limitations, LDC exports of manufactures had been admitted duty-free. U.S. imports from the five had come to account for about three-fifths of U.S. non-oil purchases from developing countries. Similar action had been taken by the European Community at the beginning of 1981.

The progressive dismantling of trade restrictions following World War II and the resultant rapid growth of world trade were a key factor in the

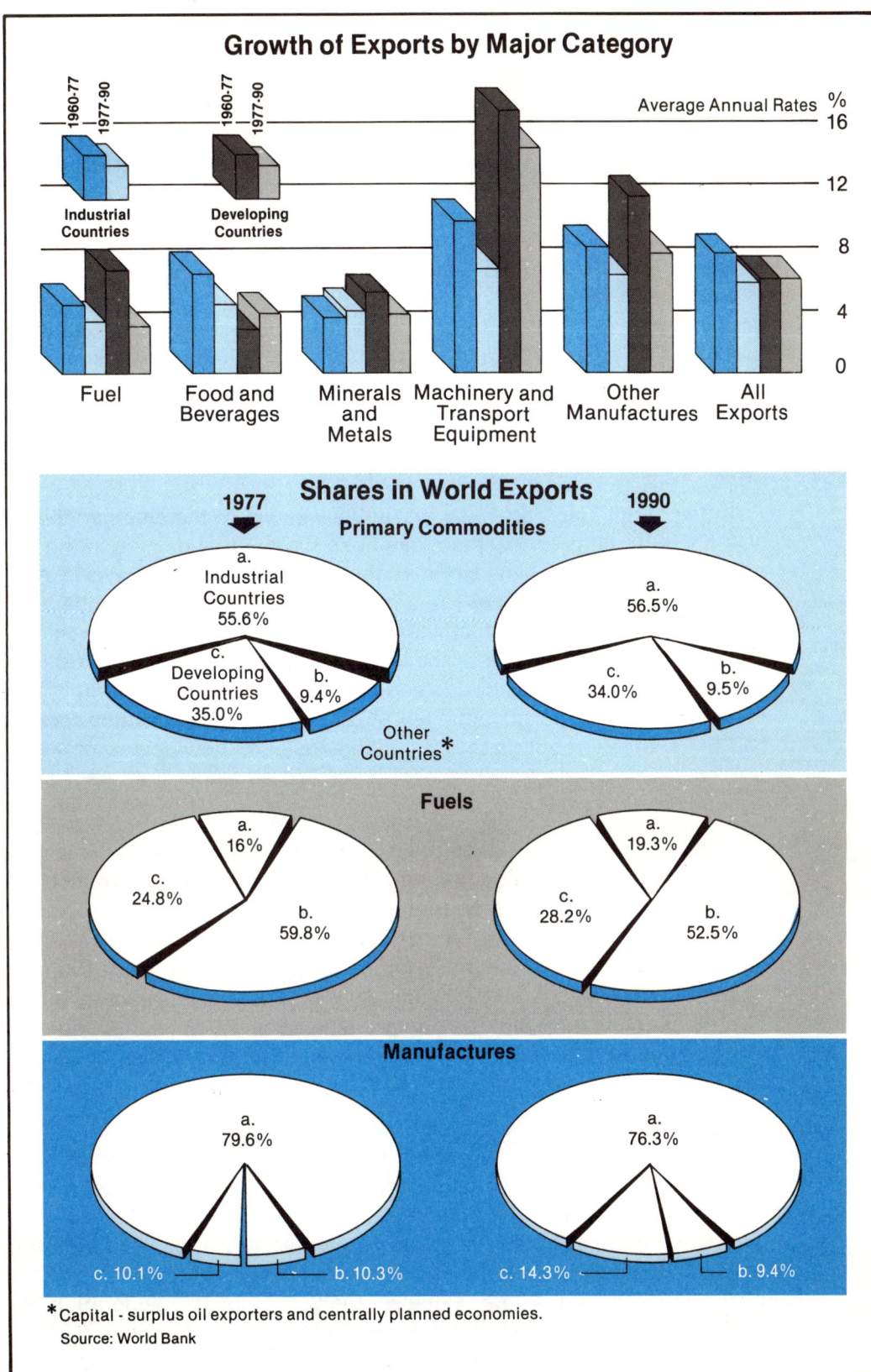

worldwide rise in prosperity during the early postwar decades. But during the 1970's, the world's trading arrangements came under increasing pressure. It has been said that "protectionism is one of the hardiest of the economic perennials; it thrives in hard times." Thus, as economic growth slowed, unemployment rose, and the payments position of the major oil importers deteriorated, protectionist sentiment began to strengthen once more.

In addition, certain structural difficulties in key industries encouraged the view that market-sharing agreements among countries might be able to ease the burden of adjustment. The general trade climate thus has become more clouded and the openness of the system more fragile. This has occurred despite the achievements of the multilateral trade negotiations (the so-called Tokyo Round) concluded in 1979, and despite repeated official pledges to the cause of economic liberalism and "free trade," the last of which was made by the OECD governments in mid-1980.

An important—and probably inevitable—cause of the emergence of a less liberal trading environment has been the gradual decline in the role of the United States in the world economy. In the early post-World War II period, the United States was in a position to promote a more liberal trading order without much concern for reciprocity. As imports constituted only a small share of the U.S. market, the growth in imports through freer trade was not deemed disruptive. At the same time, foreign demand for U.S. exports continued strong as foreign production facilities had to be largely rebuilt and U.S. technology and know-how were highly welcome. Thus, open trade was not perceived as much of a threat by either side.

In the mid-1970's, the focus of protectionist moves both in the United States and Europe were on labor-intensive industries that were feeling strong competition from the rapidly industrializing third-world countries, particularly in such sectors as textiles and consumer electronics. These industries, along with steel and shipbuilding, persuaded their governments to erect various protectionist devices. Subsequent manifestations of protectionism reflected the rising price of energy, as in the automobile industry where fuel efficiency became the overriding competitive factor.

How large is this current protectionist surge, which has been characterized by the use of nontariff restrictions, in contrast to the "old" protectionism that relied primarily on tariffs? A recent estimate by the secretariat of GATT (General Agreement on Tariffs and Trade) has suggested that import barriers in the industrial countries were affecting between 3 and 5 percent of all international trade or, for 1980, some $50 billion to $80 billion. A more detailed analysis by the Confederation of British Industry indicates that between 1974 and 1979 "managed," that is, controlled, trade rose from 40 to 46 percent for the world as a whole

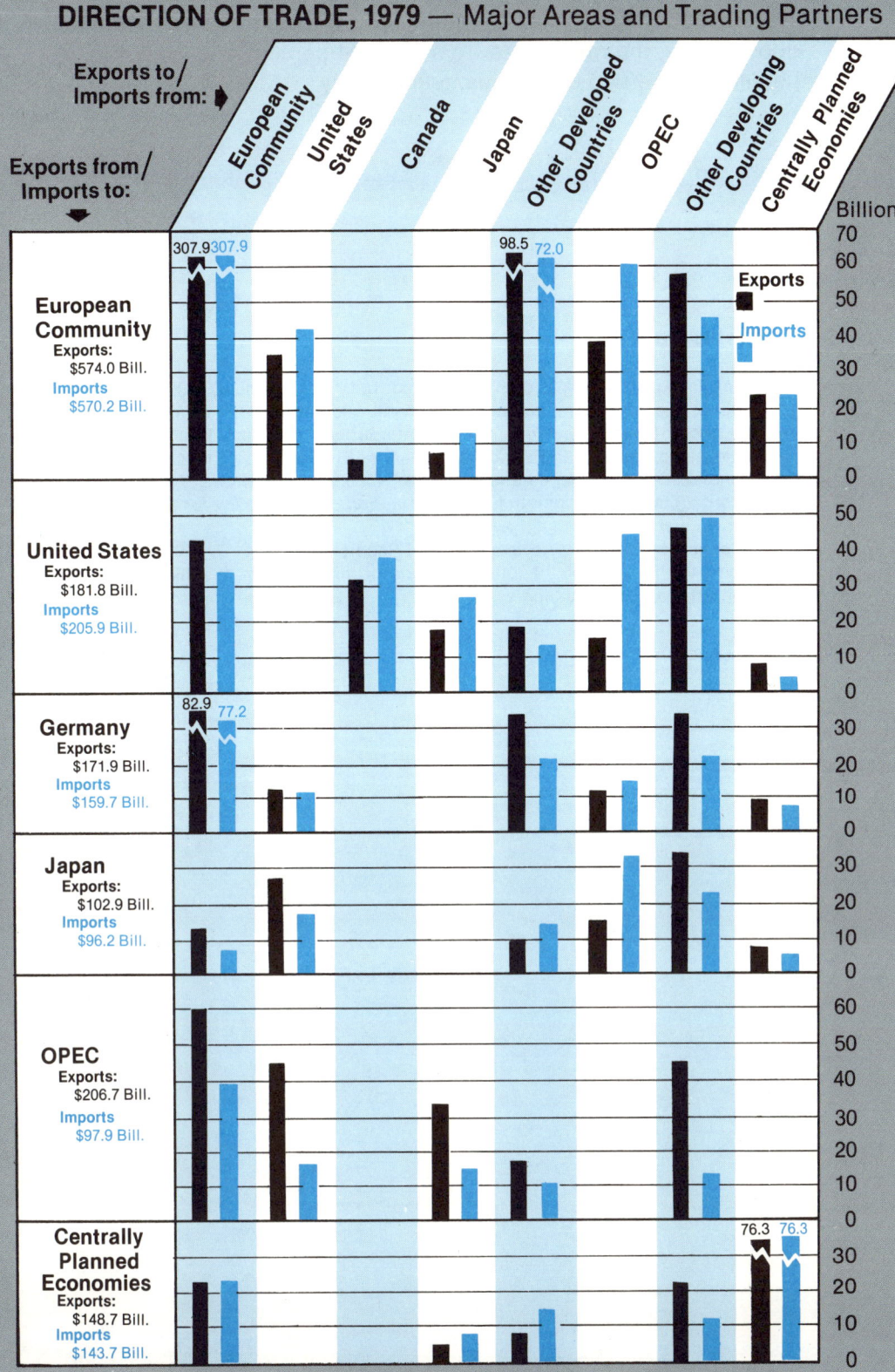

and from 36 to 42 percent for the industrial countries. For manufactured goods alone, the ratios rose from 13 to 21 percent and from 4 to 15 percent for the two categories, respectively.

Bibliography

The Banker, "Sliding into an undeclared trade war." August, 1980.

Burki, Shahid J., "The prospects for the developing world: a review of recent forecasts." *Finance and Development* (International Monetary Fund), March, 1981.

Cleveland, Harold van B. and Ramachandra Bhagavatula, "The Continuing World Economic Crisis." America and the World, 1980. *Foreign Affairs,* Vol. 59., No. 3.

Confederation of British Industry, *International Trade Policy for the 1980's.* London: August, 1980.

Council of Economic Advisers, Annual Report, Chapter 4, "The World Economy: Coping With Transition." *Economic Report of the President,* Washington: Government Printing Office, January, 1981.

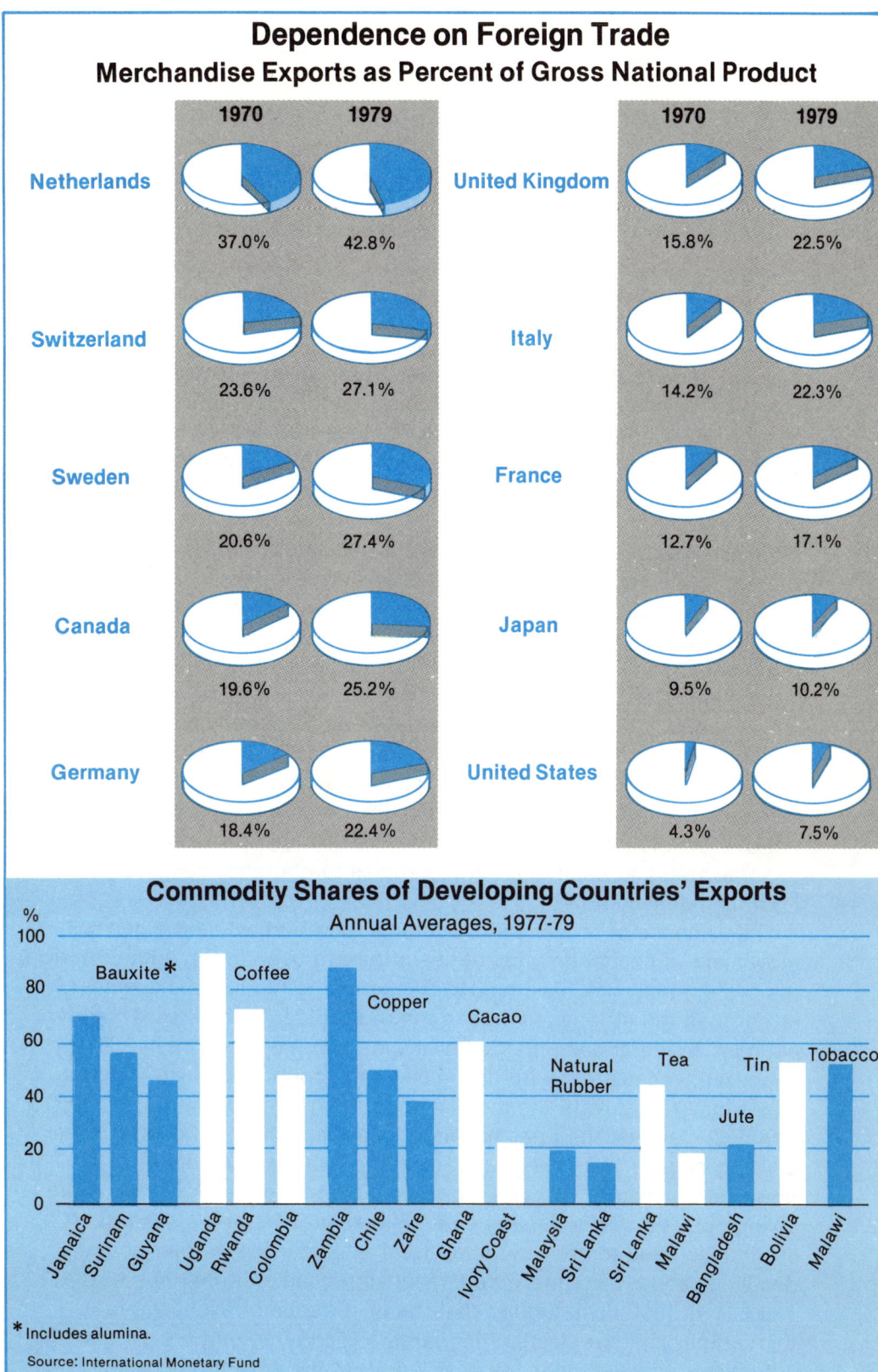

International Payments

The evolution of the international monetary system since the late 1960's has reflected deliberately planned changes only to a limited extent. Rather, what modifications have taken place have largely been a result of the pressure of economic forces. For example, it was primarily the wide disparities in economic performance among countries, especially as regards inflation, and the attendant failure to make the proper exchange-rate adjustments that led to the breakdown of the Bretton Woods system in the early 1970's and to the floating-rate system of today.

While the present exchange-rate arrangements clearly are more flexible than the fixed or par-value system that prevailed for almost 30 years after World War II, they cannot be characterized with precision. A large number of countries still peg their currencies to the dollar, to some other currency, or to some composite basket of currencies such as the Special Drawing Rights (SDR's). But these various arrangements—which include the linked rates of the European Monetary System for all members of the European Community, except the United Kingdom—are not overly significant in global terms. The bulk of world trade is still denominated and conducted in currencies that are not pegged and are floating independently.

The evidence of recent years demonstrates that, while the general movement of exchange rates appears to have been in the right direction, the system may well have tended to encourage too much movement, rather than too little, as had been the case under fixed rates. Thus, rate changes have not been gradual over time, nor have they been necessarily consistent with divergences in economic activity among countries. Rather, with the increasing internationalization of the world's financial markets, the rates for major currencies have tended to move abruptly as well as to overreact quickly to changed perceptions of financial prospects. This has led to acceptance of the view that, while giving due rein to the influence of basic economic forces, monetary authorities need to consider short-term rate changes in their policy decisions and hence intervene in exchange markets from time to time.

It has, in fact, been argued that the occurrence of exchange-rate fluctuations that are deemed too large and too frequent proves that the adjustment process does not work and that the advent of floating rates

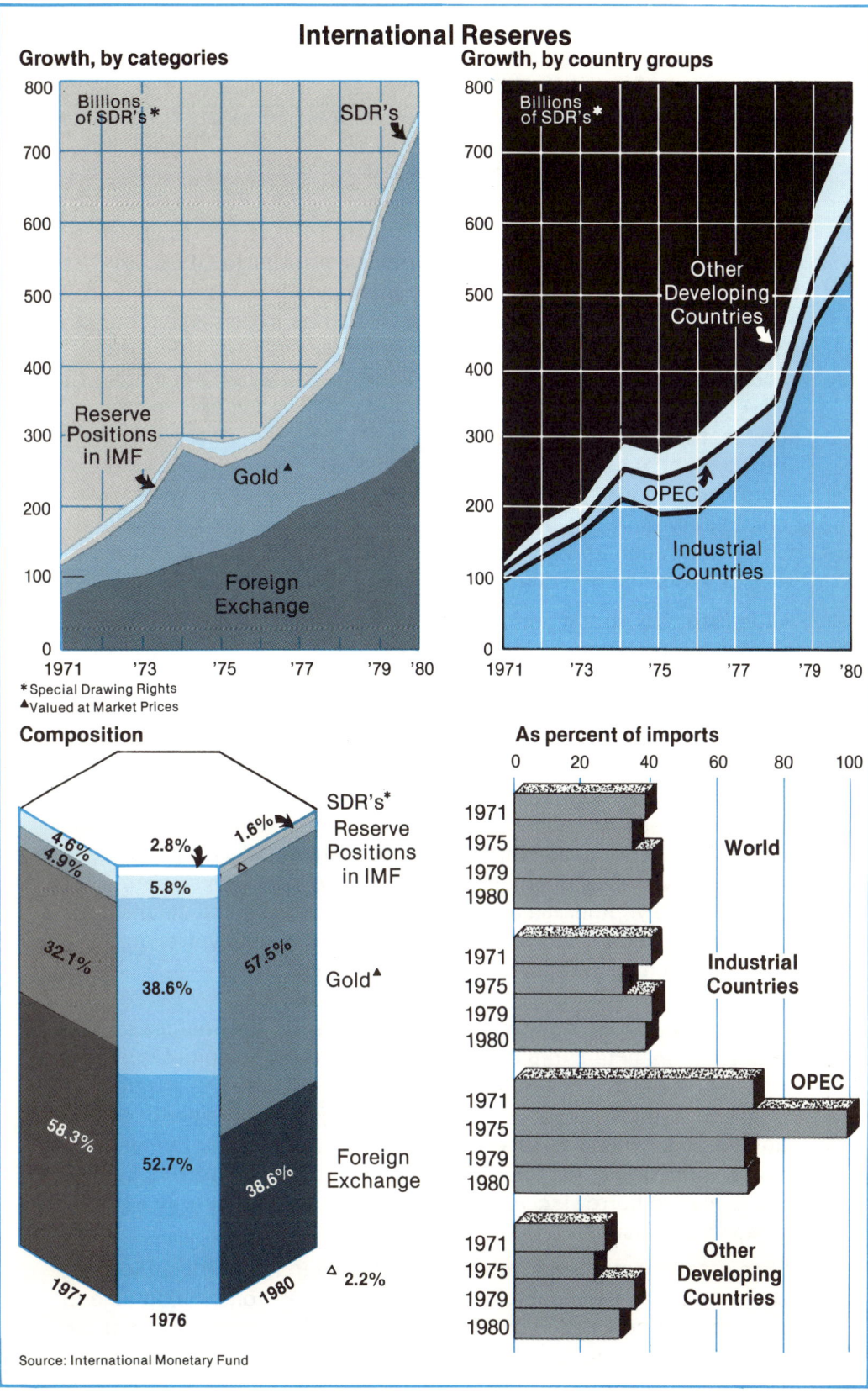

has actually hindered, rather than promoted, international adjustment. Some would even argue that the present arrangements are no system at all, since they are not formalized in the neat fashion of Bretton Woods. The majority view, however, is that the system does work and that the adjustments that took place in the mid-and late 1970's must be considered major achievements of the world economy.

More specifically, the system weathered the oil price shock of 1973-1974, which abruptly altered the global pattern of current-account balances by massive transfers of purchasing power to OPEC. The system again worked successfully in more recent years, when it appeared as though Germany and Japan would be in permanent surplus and the United States in permanent deficit. In 1980, the U.S. current account achieved balance for the second year in a row—despite a rise of over $40 billion in U.S. oil imports since 1978—and became the strongest within OECD. Japan and Germany, on the other hand, moved into substantial deficit in both 1979 and 1980. These changes have, of course, been both cyclical and energy-related, but they also reflect coordinated efforts by the countries concerned to correct their external positions through appropriate domestic economic policies and the effects of exchange-rate changes.

The resultant strong performance of the dollar has removed much of the earlier motivation for moving out of dollars—the so-called diversification motive—which only a few years ago was seen as a major factor encouraging increased use of other currencies in international finance. The dollar remains the predominant currency in international trade, as well as the currency in which the bulk of international financial transactions are dominated. Thus, in 1980 more than two-thirds of Eurobond issues and some 95 percent of medium-term Eurocurrency credits were dollar denominated. So also were about 72 percent of all Eurocurrency credits outstanding at the end of 1980. Thus, both singly and collectively, other major currencies still play a much smaller international role than the dollar and a true multicurrency system, although much discussed, is far from a reality.

During the 1970's, significant shifts occurred in the sources of international financing, in parallel with the rapid expansion of international financial markets. While borrowing from both official and private sources continued to grow, the latter source gained greatly in importance. In addition, there was a relative shift away from both direct foreign investment (which is not included in debt statistics) and private suppliers' credits toward borrowing via financial markets—that is, from banks and through bond issues.

The greatly increased involvement of banks in international lending, especially to the developing countries; the strong competition among them; and the prevalence of a borrower's market through much of the period since 1974 have given rise to some concern among observers of

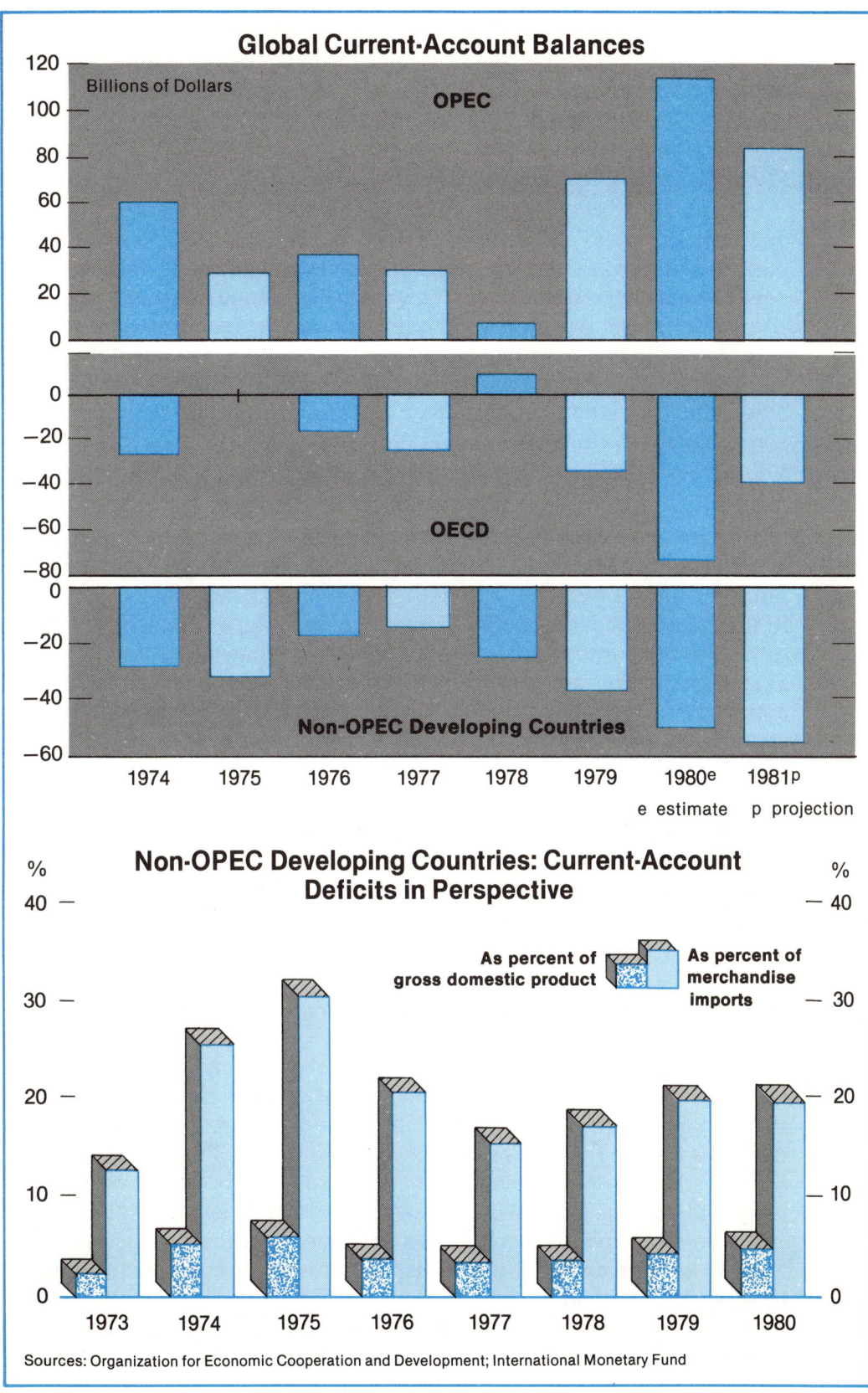

international financial developments. Banks have, for good reasons, become more aware of such matters as the external debt situation of borrowers, the degree of concentration in country exposure, and the adequacy of their capital base. Indeed, it has been remarked that "under present conditions the equity of the international banks is the keystone of the international financial system."

However, in answering the question of whether individual countries may have borrowed excessively, banks obviously look beyond various statistical indicators to a country's economic management and its political and social framework. Thus, the more cautious attitude recently adopted by banks toward their international lending suggests that their contribution to the recycling of the latest oil-related payments deficits may be relatively less significant than it was after 1973-1974. On the other hand, the various official channels and institutions are expected to play a more important role.

For the non-OPEC developing countries, the shift from official to private sources of credit over the past decade has brought with it an appreciable increase in both interest and amortization payments, over and above the general rise in interest rates. In the average debt-service ratios for the entire group of countries, moreover, heavy weight is given to the major exporters of manufactured goods, whose own debt-service ratios are comparatively low and, because of the buoyancy of their exports, have not risen very much. On the other hand, interest and amortization payments of the so-called low-income countries have risen sharply.

The development of international bank credit available to a wide range of countries, including many developing ones, has had another notable effect. It has reduced the difference between the United States, on the one hand, and many other countries, on the other, as regards their ability to finance a payments deficit. Thus, it is not now only the United States that can finance such a deficit by issuing liabilities expressed in dollars. Most other countries can do likewise by using the credit facilities of the world banking system.

This arrangement does not mean, of course, that any country can finance unlimited deficits through the use of dollar borrowings, but for many countries the amounts so available are larger than otherwise would be the case. Nor does it mean that the United States need not be concerned about the amount of dollars it issues to finance its own payments deficits. But the previously existing asymmetry in the system has been somewhat tempered, because other countries have been relieved to some extent of the necessity to settle an external imbalance by drawing down their reserves.

Against this background, the urgency to overhaul the international monetary system—mainly by shifting away from reliance on the dollar as

FOREIGN EXCHANGE RATES

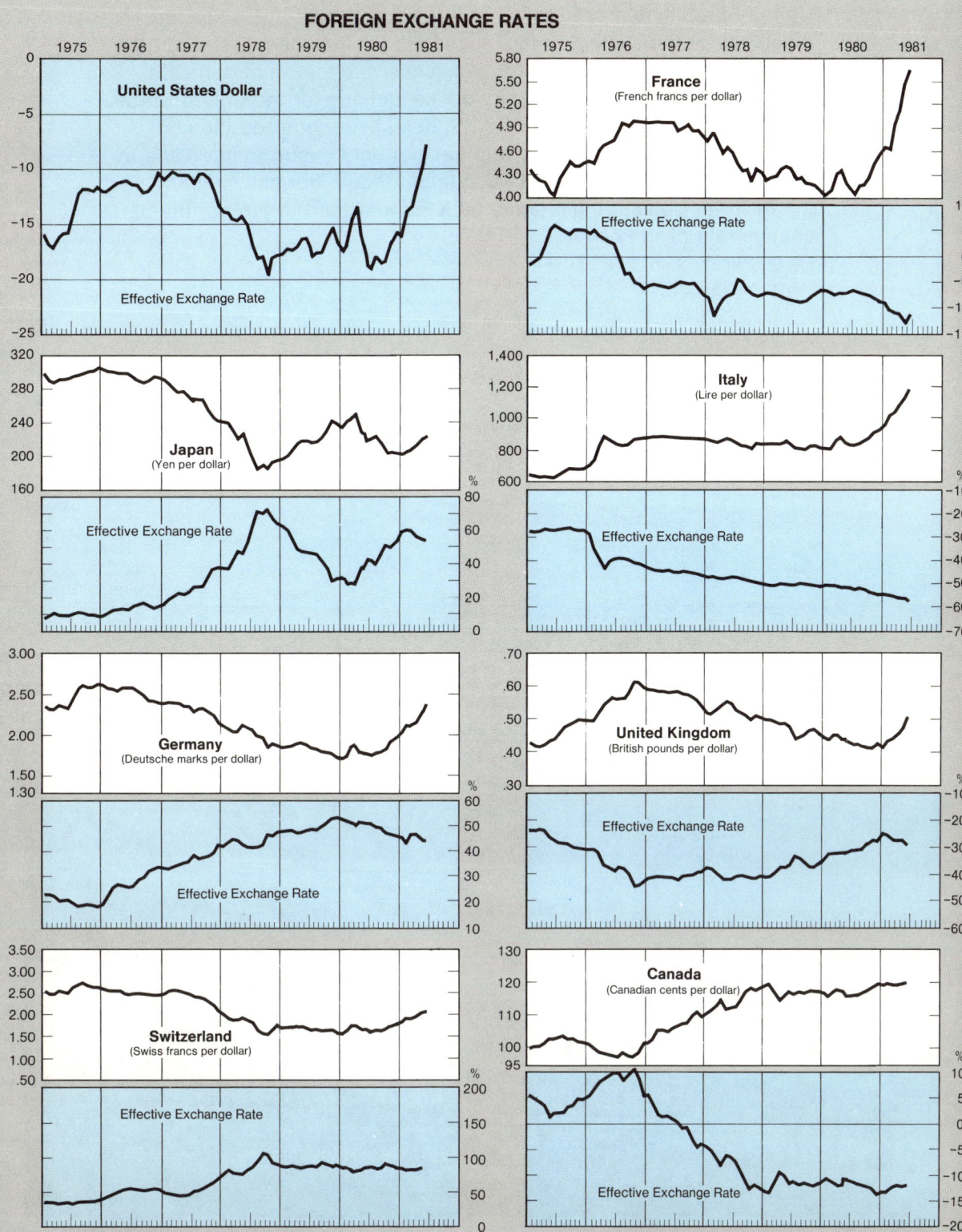

Effective Exchange Rate for each country indicates changes vis-a-vis a group of 15 major currencies, weighted according to the average bilateral manufactures trade of 1976. Changes are in percent from pre-June 1970 parities, based on monthly average of daily rates.

Source: Morgan Guaranty Trust.

the chief means of settlement—has lessened. At the same time, the United States has moved to accept, at least in part, the so-called discipline of the system. It has accepted, for instance, that a strong depreciation of the dollar, through excessive creation of domestic liquidity, has serious inflationary consequences for the United States. Since November, 1978, the United States has recognized the consequence of this relationship and has not only begun to intervene in exchange markets with assets acquired abroad, but has similarly seen the need for domestic monetary policies that tend to protect the exchange rate of the dollar.

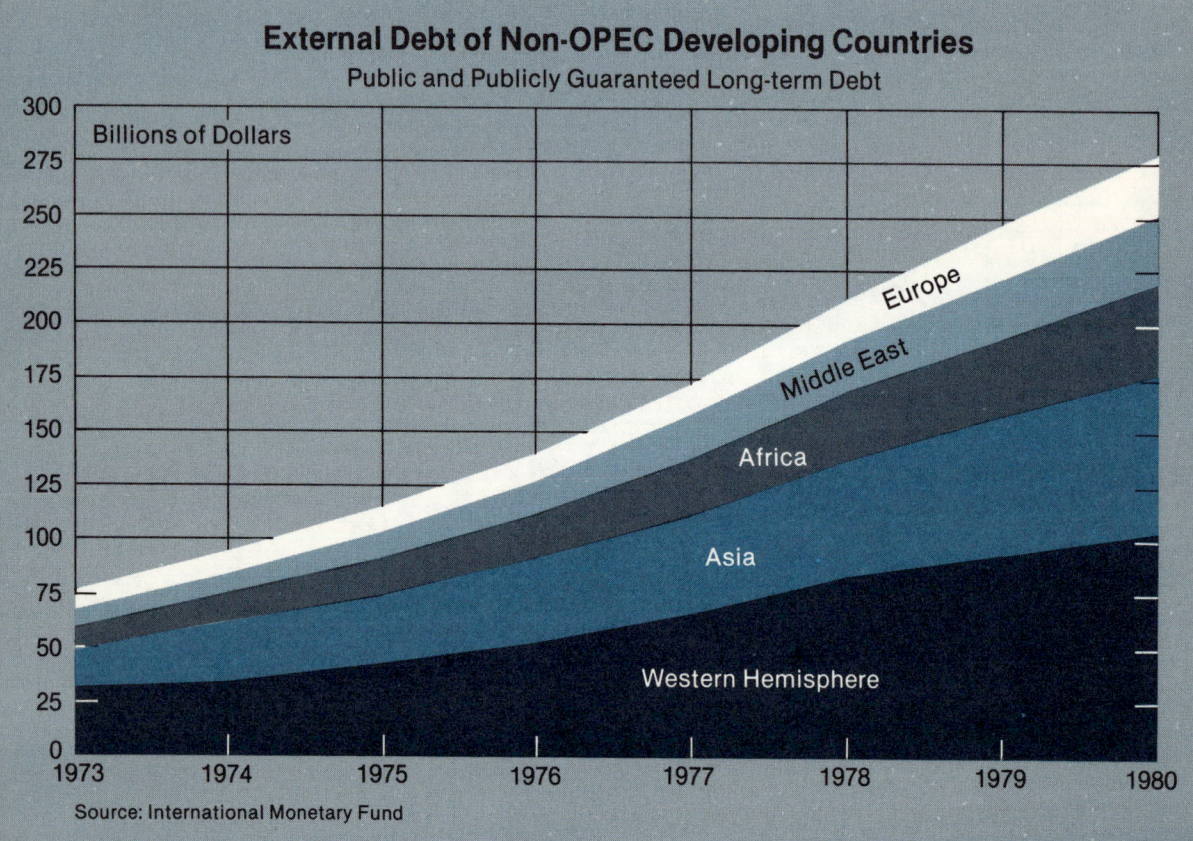

Bibliography

Atlantic Council of the United States, *The International Monetary System in Transition.* Policy Papers, Washington: May, 1980.

Bergsten, Fred C., "The International Monetary System in the 1980's," *new international realities.* Washington: National Planning Association, March, 1981.

Bouey, Gerald K., "The International Monetary System: Key Issues," paper delivered at the 33rd International Banking Summer School, Banff, Alberta, September 1, 1980. Ottawa: Bank of Canada, mimeographed.

Friedman, Irving S., "The Role of Private Banks in Stabilization Programs," in William R. Cline and Sidney Weintraub, eds., *Economic Stabilization in Developing Countries.* Washington: The Brookings Institution, 1981.

Hein, John, "OPEC Surpluses, Recycling, and the Dollar," *The Bankers Magazine,* January-February, 1981.

Pringle, Robin, "The shape of currency crises in the 1980's," *The Banker,* February, 1981.

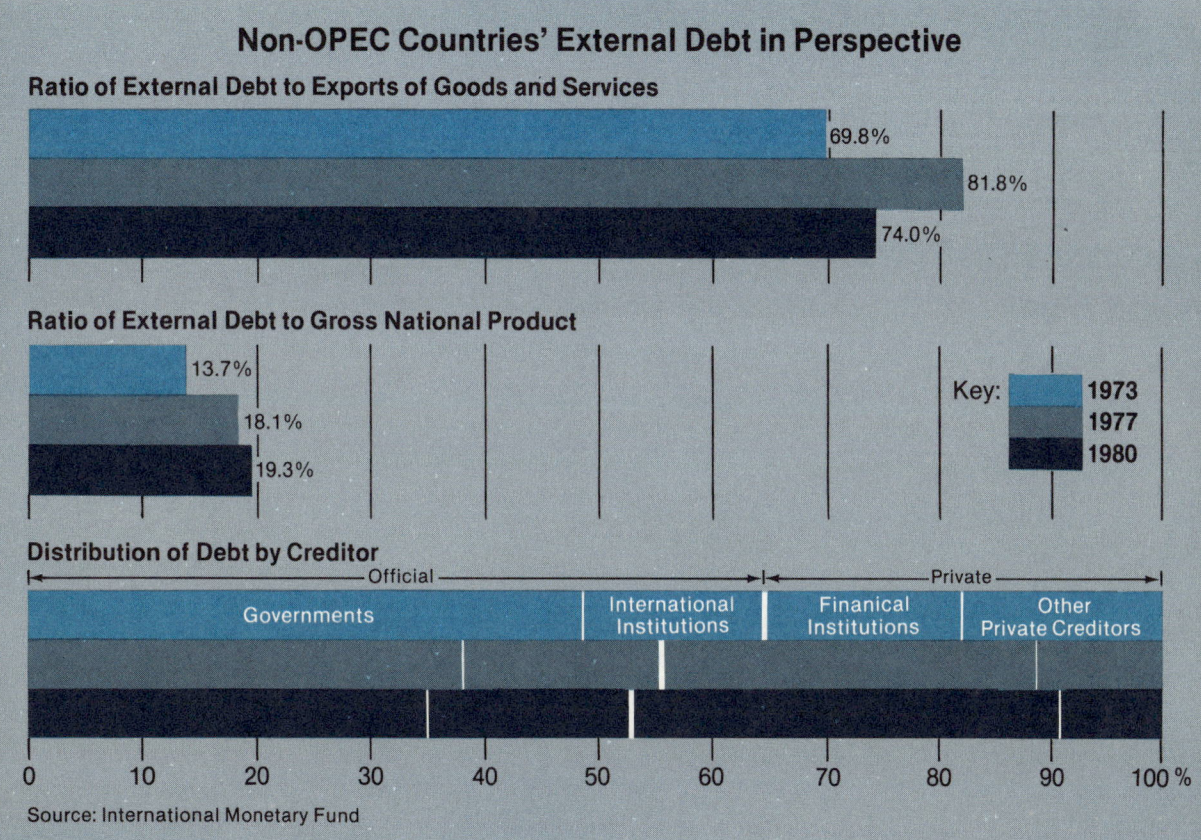

Energy

The steep rise in oil prices since 1973 has probably been the most dramatic factor dominating the world economy as well as economic thinking and policymaking in the past decade. The statistics are well known by now. Crude oil prices quadrupled in 1973-1974 and rose by another 150 percent in 1979-1980. In real terms, the price of imported oil rose by more than 300 percent between 1972 and late 1980 for the member countries of the Organization for Economic Cooperation and Development (OECD).

These sharp increases—equal to about 2 percent of OECD gross national product in 1973-1974 and again in 1979-1980—have had two

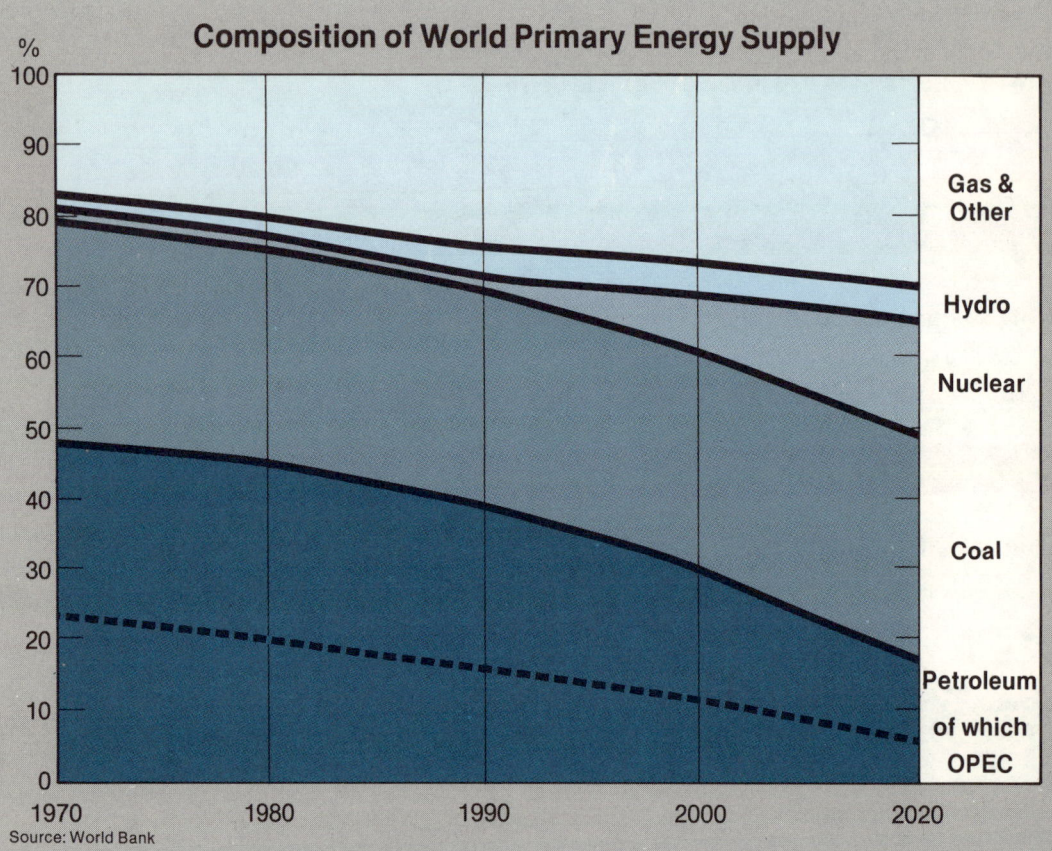

marked effects. They were deflationary by transferring spending power from oil-importing to oil-exporting countries—at least, until the latter began using their new wealth to boost their imports of goods and services. At the same time, the oil price increases were inflationary by raising the cost of energy and hence of virtually everything else in the importing countries.

By themselves, however, rising oil prices have made a much smaller contribution to domestic inflation in user countries than is commonly alleged, since the final price of oil to the consumers has risen by far less than crude oil prices. According to OECD calculations, from 1972 to

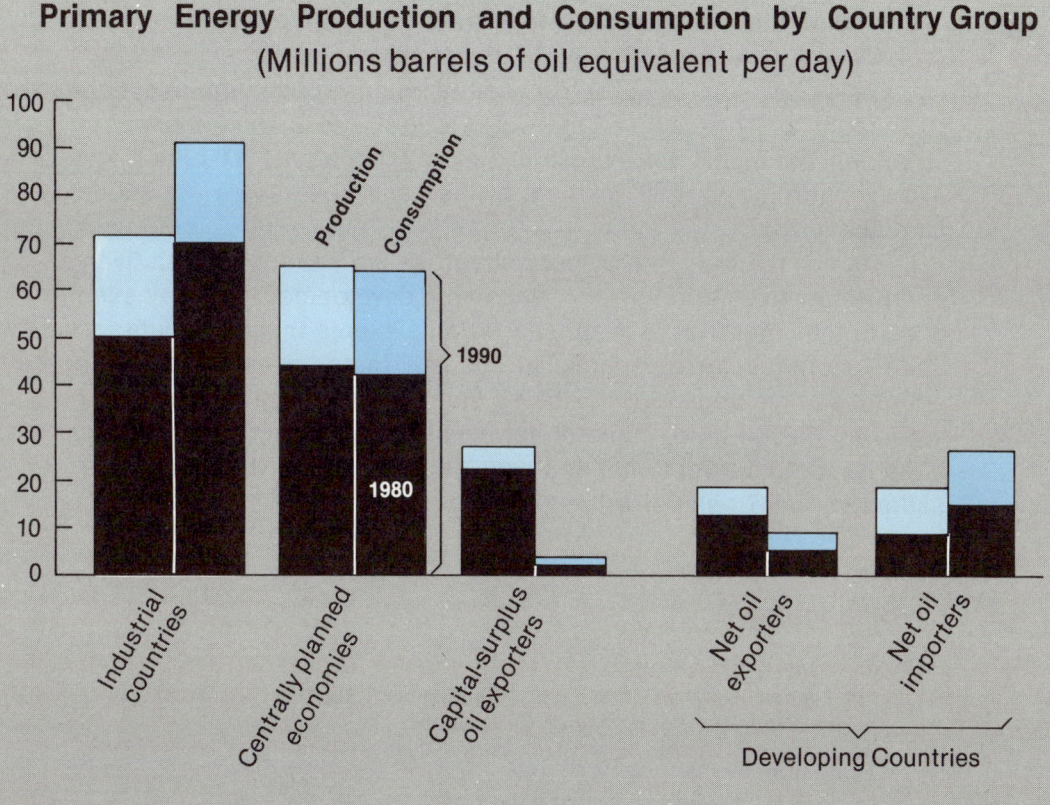

1979 the real energy price to households in OECD countries rose by only 3 percent a year and to industrial users by only 8 percent. For the period as a whole, energy prices to final users in these countries rose by 27 percent between 1972 and 1974, fell slightly in the following four years, and rose by over 30 percent since 1978. There are additional differences for individual countries, depending on how their currencies moved against the dollar.

With the real price of energy estimated to rise by a further 50 percent by the year 2000, the economic impact of energy will remain a central concern for policymakers everywhere. What happens to prices will, of course, be affected by trends in both conservation and production.

The greatest scope for conservation obviously rests with the industrial countries, which account for more than half of total world energy consumption. On average, these countries use about eight times as much commercial energy per person as the so-called middle-income countries, and more than 40 times as much as the low-income countries. This reflects not only their much greater degree of industrialization, but also the fact that both their agricultural sectors and their households are more energy intensive. But they also have been able to reduce the ratio of energy use to GNP, which fell between 7 and 16 percent in the seven major industrial countries between 1973 and 1977.

Excluding the major oil exporters, the developing countries account for only about 13 percent of world use of commercial energy. As their economies develop, however, this use is bound to rise, and is estimated to account for 17 percent of the world total by 1990. Thus, these countries' oil import bill—which in 1980 totaled about $50 billion and, on average, swallowed up 26 percent of their export earnings—is bound to increase further.

Moreover, the truly energy-poor countries are caught in a relatively energy-intensive period of their economic development, as they seek to acquire the industries and transportation systems that were built in the "rich" countries decades ago. But this very factor gives these developing countries some degree of flexibility, since their energy patterns are not yet fixed. This, in turn, militates for development of indigenous energy supplies, both conventional and novel, whose cost in the long run is estimated to be well below that of imported oil.

Bibliography

The Banker, "The wrong price for energy," August, 1980.
The Economist, "Third-world energy." September 6, 1980.
Exxon Corporation, *World Energy Outlook, 1981.*
Kredietbank (Brussels), "Energy prices over the past 25 years." *Weekly Bulletin,* April 18, 1980.
World Bank, *World Development Report, 1980.* Washington: August, 1980.

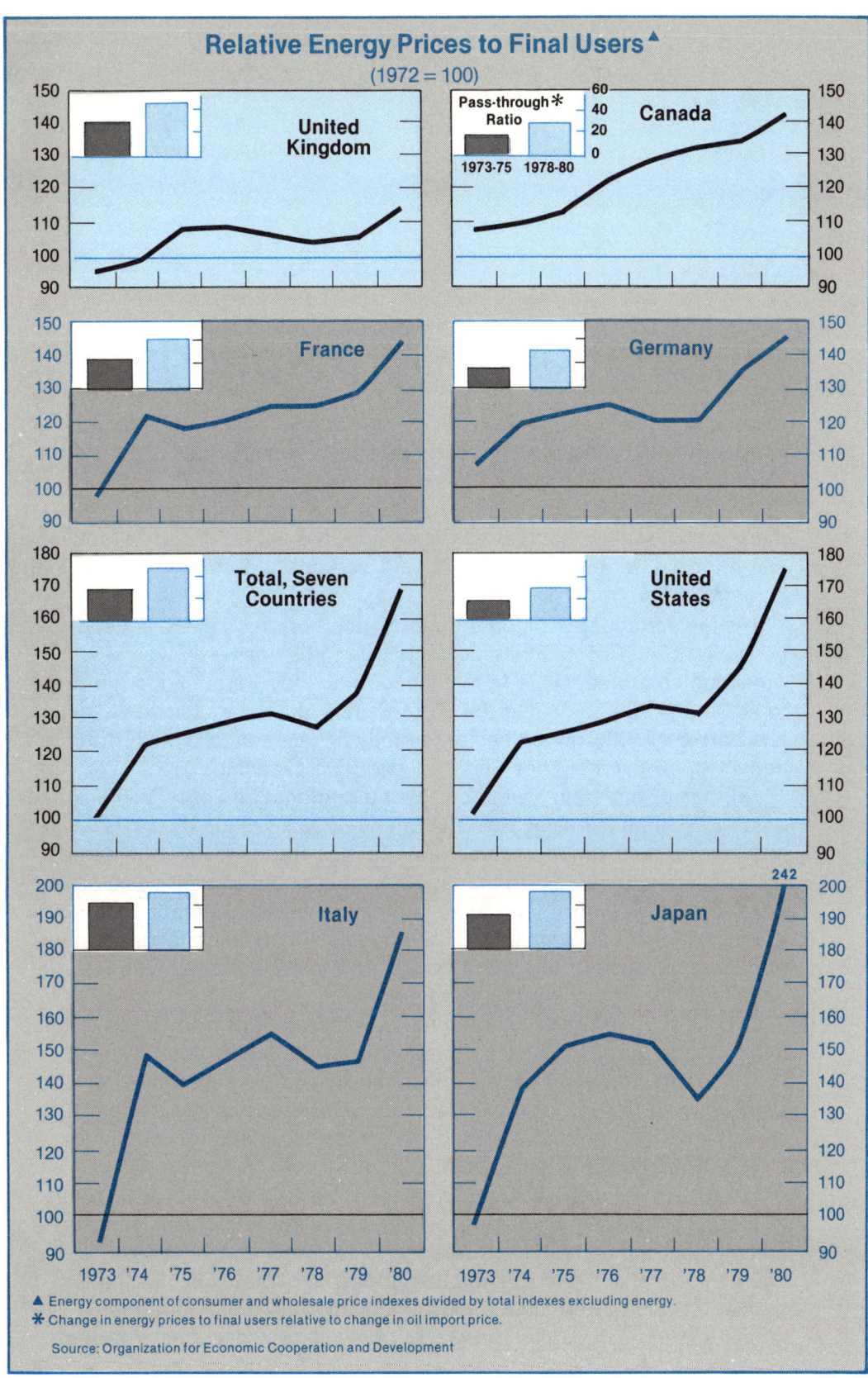

Multinational Corporations

Not too many years ago, it was an all too familiar stereotype that the multinational corporation tended to be based in the United States. This perception reflected the phenomenon of the *défi américain*, or the American challenge, formulated by Jacques Servan-Schreiber in 1968—the possibility, that is, "that the world's third greatest industrial power, just after the United States and Russia, will not be Europe, but American industry in Europe."

It is understandable that multinational corporations (MNC's) used to be seen—and in some instances continue to be seen—as typically American creatures, since in many countries they were among the first to arrive and also remained the most visible. Moreover, as one observer has noted: "U.S. firms are easier to study because data on their foreign activities are the most detailed and extensive available."

Yet, one of the main events on the international business scene of the past ten years has easily been the dramatic gains made by non-U.S. MNC's over their American counterparts. It is true that U.S. companies still predominate in certain industrial sectors and that their sales have continued to grow. But the much heralded (and much feared) domination of international business by U.S. companies simply is no longer a point of debate because of the sharp erosion of their earlier lead. The relevant data serve to underscore this development.

In 1963, U.S. MNC's accounted for two-thirds of the world's 100 largest industrial corporations and for three-fifths of the 500 largest. By 1979, that share had dropped to below one-half for each group. Similarly, a breakdown of the world's 500 largest corporations by size of sales reveals that the traditional lead in the top sales categories long enjoyed by U.S. firms disappeared by 1979.

A comparison of the aggregate sales of the 100 largest U.S. and the 100 largest non-U.S. companies, by groups of ten, tells a similar story—namely, that the combined sales of the U.S. firms relative to their foreign counterparts also have been declining steadily. Total sales for the ten largest U.S. firms were about two-and-a-half times those of the ten largest foreign companies in 1963, but only slightly over one-and-a-half

The World's 100 and 500 Largest Industrial Corporations by Nationality

Number of Companies

1963

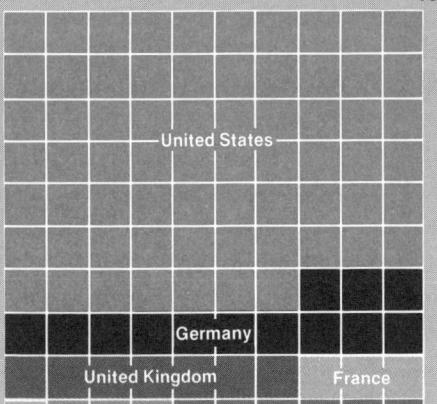
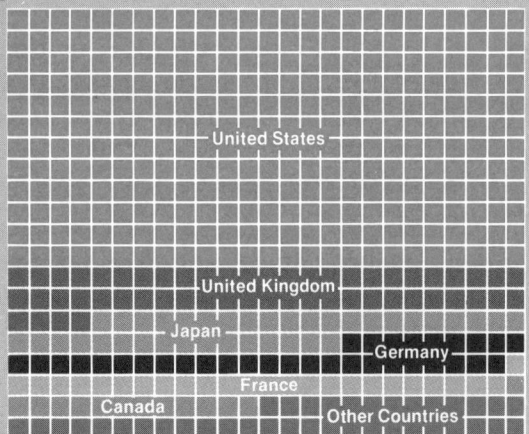

1971

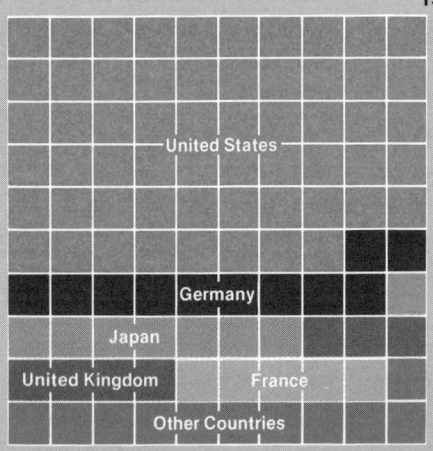
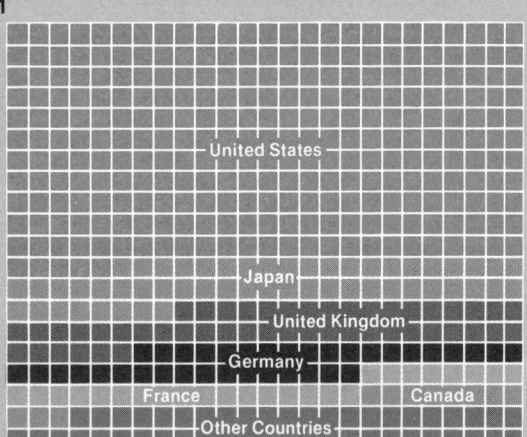

1979

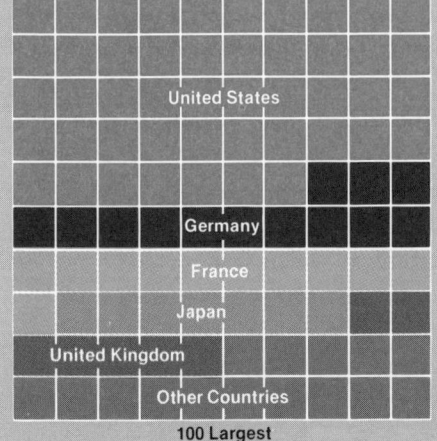
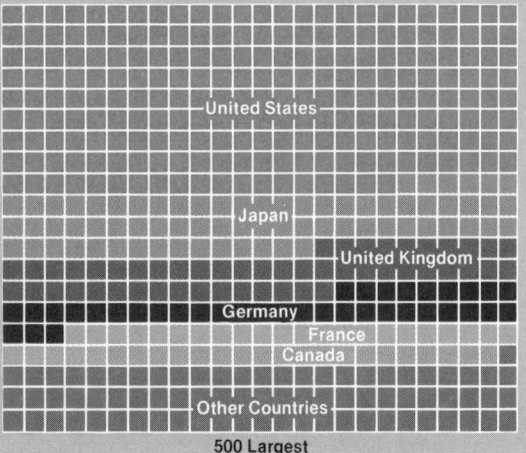

100 Largest   500 Largest

Source: *Fortune*

times in 1979. Correspondingly, the U.S. lead, or share, had dwindled in major industry groups—although the results predictably vary from industry to industry.

The reasons behind this relative decline of U.S. MNC's are several. They include the loss of U.S. predominance in technology transfer; the steady growth of European and Japanese firms' capability to innovate; the faster rise of European and Japanese exports, with production abroad usually following in their wake; and the greater adaptability, both politically and economically, of foreign MNC's to the needs of host countries.

The last-named factor has been particularly pronounced in the field of energy-saving equipment. As one author has noted, it is not surprising that, as the cost of energy has risen, European companies such as Michelin should be building factories in the United States to produce radial tires; that Robert Bosch should be manufacturing fuel-injection equipment in the United States; or that Pechiney should be increasing its U.S. market share because of its electricity-saving smelting of aluminum. Non-U.S. companies similarly are considered ahead of their U.S. counterparts in nuclear and other energy technologies designed to cope with resource scarcities as well as in the development of pollution control, recycling and conservation devices.

Another recent trend among the world's multinationals has been the rise in foreign investments by firms from developing countries (LDC's). In addition to companies from OPEC countries and to firms based in tax havens, multinationals have emerged in Argentina, Brazil, Colombia, Hong Kong, India, Korea and the Philippines. Much of their international activity has been directed to other developing countries. According to one observer, companies from Asian LDC's together account for more investment in Indonesia (except in mining and petroleum) than Japanese, North American, or European investment. This strong preference may well indicate that for developing countries seeking foreign management and technology, such investment by other LDC's offers "a politically and perhaps economically attractive alternative to the multinational enterprise."

A third and fairly recent phenomenon is that, with the emergence of non-U.S. MNC's, host countries have been able to deal with a greater diversity of foreign companies. This enables them to compare the investing companies' political and economic advantages, weigh the relative costs, and "play them off" against each other. In fact, today virtually no country, industrial or developing, finds itself playing host to multinationals from one single home country. In addition, alternative forms of business organization—such as banks, retailers, consulting firms, and trading companies—have come to the fore as carriers for the transmittal of technology and other types of know-how.

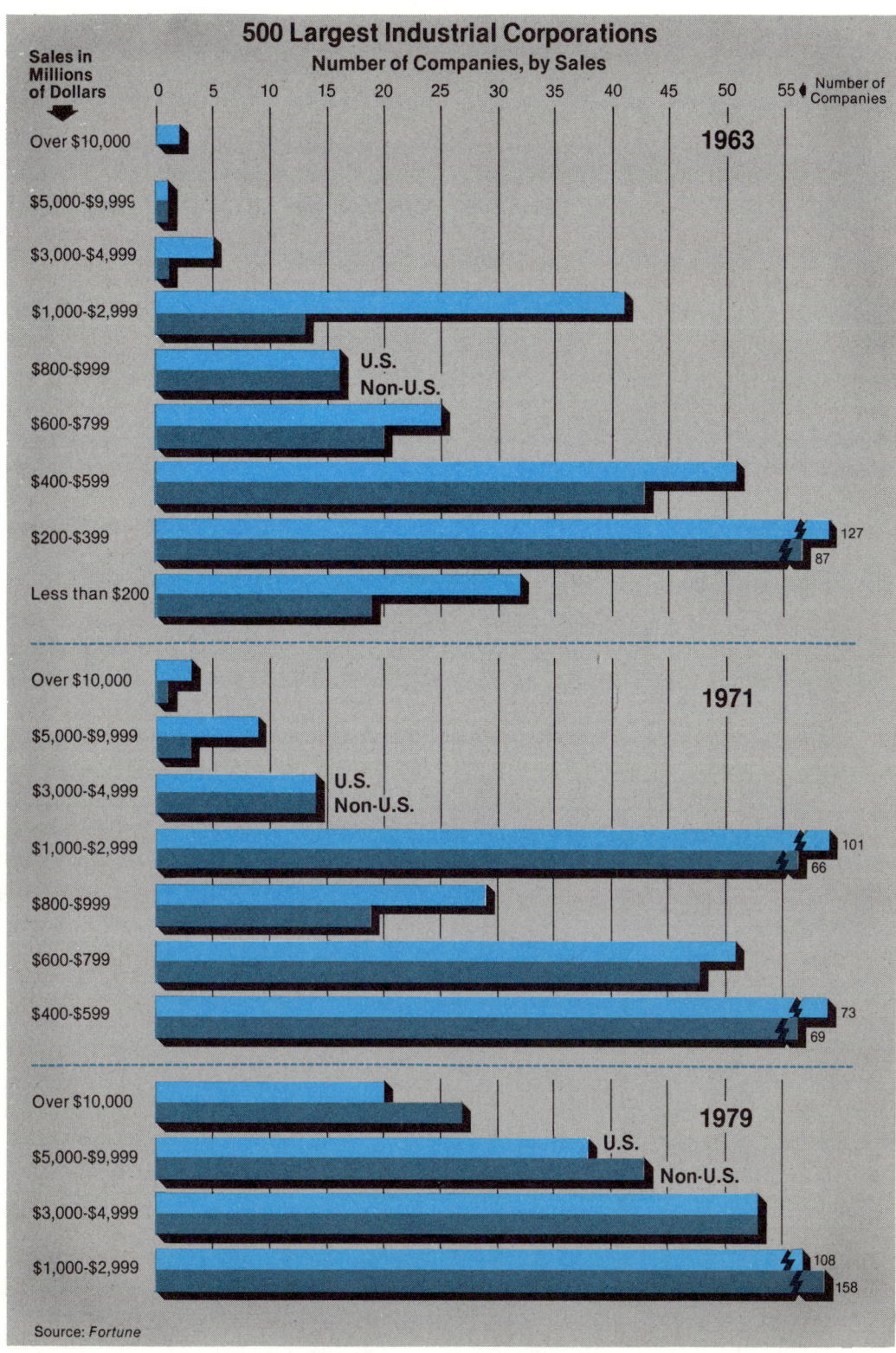

Finally, competition from state-trading companies in developing countries, from state-trading activities in socialist economies, and from nationally owned or closely controlled enterprises in major European countries are all bringing about further fundamental changes in global trading and investment patterns. Not too long ago, it had been predicted that with the inexorable rise of the MNC's the nation-state would find itself "at bay" and might eventually wither away completely. However, its obituaries appear to have been premature and accommodation, rather than confrontation, between national sovereignty and the large international corporation increasingly appears to be the order of the day.

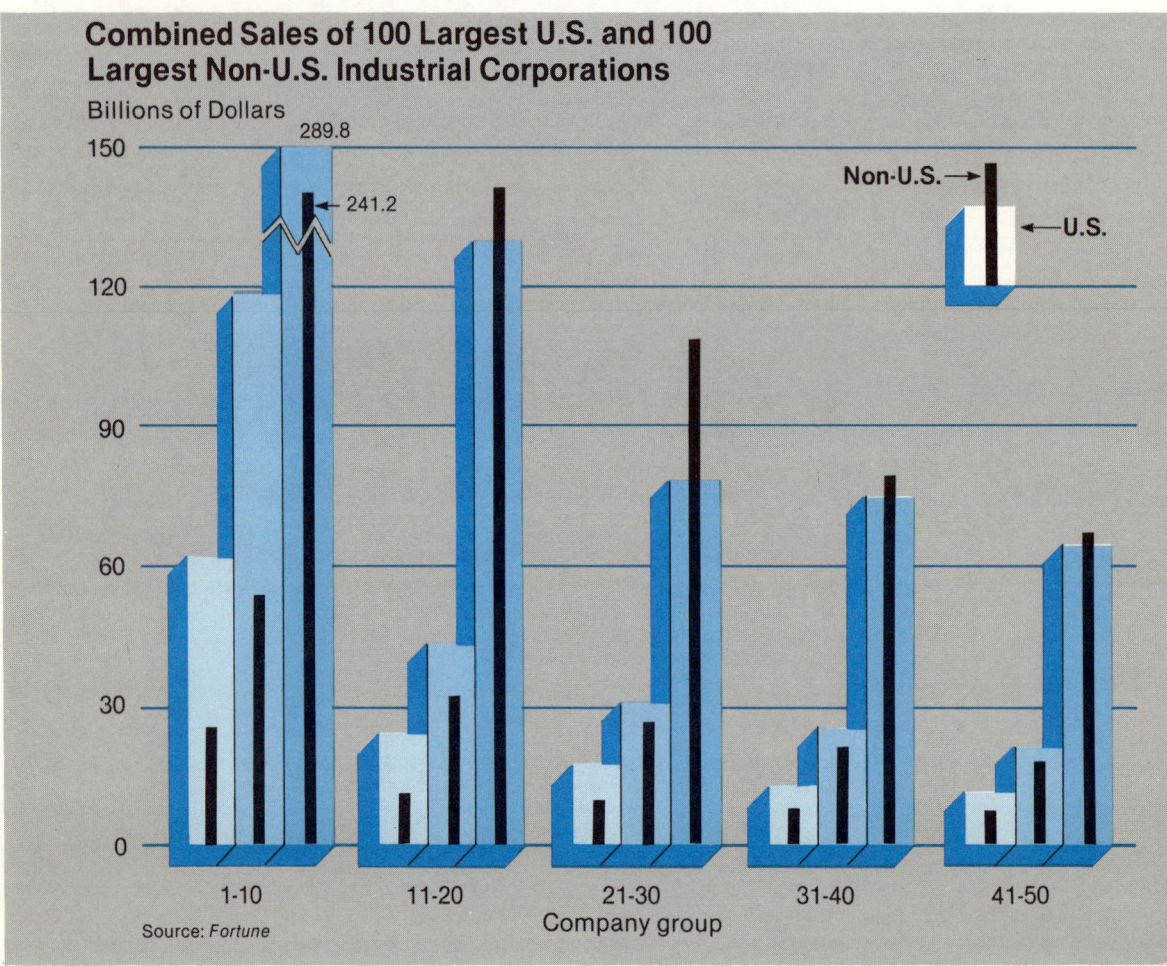

Bibliography

Aharoni, Yair, "The State-Owned Enterprise as a Competitor in International Markets." *Columbia Journal of World Business,* Spring, 1980.

Franko, Lawrence G., "Multinationals: the end of U.S. dominance." *Harvard Business Review,* November-December, 1978.

Heenan, David A. and Warren J. Keegan, "The Rise of Third-World Multinationals." *Harvard Business Review,* January-February, 1979.

Hein, John, *The World's Multinationals: A Global Challenge.* The Conference Board, Information Bulletin No. 84, 1981.

Streeten, Paul, "Multinationals revisited." *Finance and Development* (International Monetary Fund), June, 1979.

Wells, Louis T. Jr., "The Internationalization of Firms from Developing Countries," in Tamir Agnon and Charles P. Kindleberger, eds., *Multinationals From Small Countries.* Cambridge, Mass.: The M.I.T. Press, 1977.

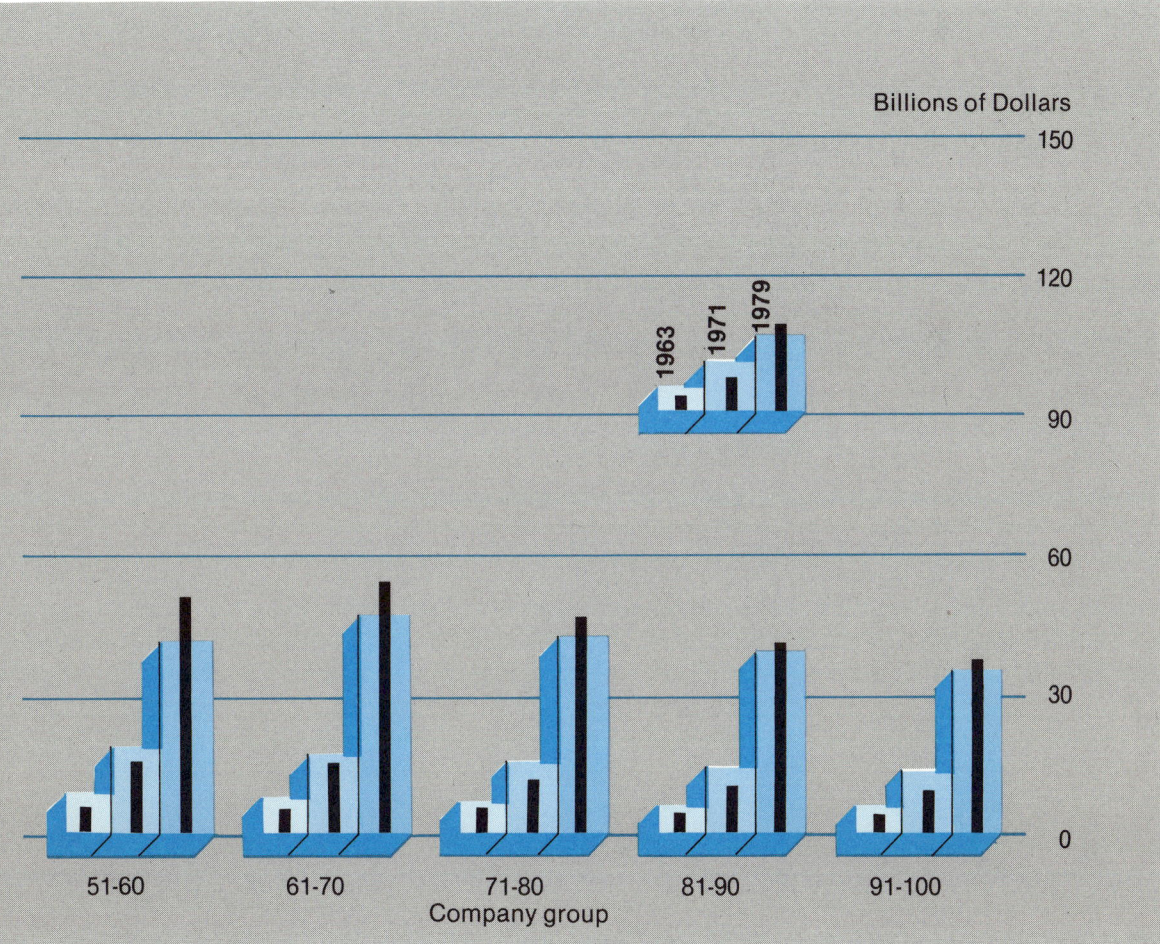